ARTS AND CRAFTS
STAINED GLASS PATTERN BOOK

CAROLYN RELEI

DOVER PUBLICATIONS, INC.
MINEOLA, NEW YORK

Bibliographical Note

Arts and Crafts Stained Glass Pattern Book is a new work, first published by Dover Publications, Inc., in 2002.

DOVER *Pictorial Archive* SERIES

This book belongs to the Dover Pictorial Archive Series. You may use the designs and illustrations for graphics and crafts applications, free and without special permission, provided that you include no more than four in the same publication or project. (For permission for additional use, please write to Permissions Department, Dover Publications, Inc., 31 East 2nd Street, Mineola, N.Y. 11501.)

However, republication or reproduction of any illustration by any other graphic service, whether it be in a book or in any other design resource, is strictly prohibited.

Library of Congress Cataloging-in-Publication Data

Relei, Carolyn.
    Arts and crafts stained glass pattern book / Carolyn Relei.
        p. cm. — (Dover pictorial archive series)
    ISBN 0-486-42318-2 (pbk.)
    1. Glass painting and staining—Patterns. 2. Arts and crafts movement.
I. Title. II. Series.

TT298 .R398 2002
748.5'028'2—dc21

2002067476

Manufactured in the United States of America
Dover Publications, Inc., 31 East 2nd Street, Mineola, N.Y. 11501

PUBLISHER'S NOTE

THE ARTS AND CRAFTS MOVEMENT, which originated in England during the latter half of the nineteenth century, began as a protest against the techniques of mass production brought about by the Industrial Revolution. Largely inspired by English artist and craftsman William Morris, the Arts and Crafts movement rejected the Victorian opulence of machine-made goods. Proponents of the Arts and Crafts movement stressed a return to the principles of craftsmanship, as practiced in the Middle Ages. This simpler decorative style soon renewed public interest in handcrafted designs. Despite the speed and availability of mass-produced items, the movement witnessed a revival in the production of handmade jewelry, wallpaper, textiles, books, and decorative metalwork. The sixty plates in this book, suitable for any number of stained glass projects, may be reproduced in larger or smaller sizes.

This collection of patterns is intended as a supplement to stained glass instruction books (such as *Stained Glass Craft* by J. A. F. Divine and G. Blachford, Dover Publications, Inc., 0-486-22812-6). All materials needed, including general instructions and tools for beginners, can usually be purchased from local craft and hobby stores listed in your Yellow Pages.

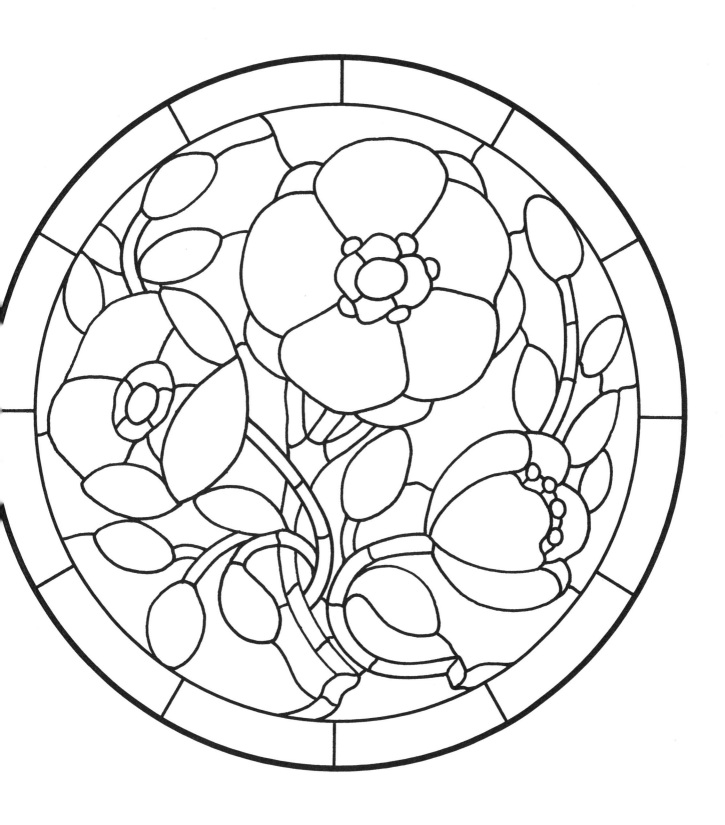

3

4

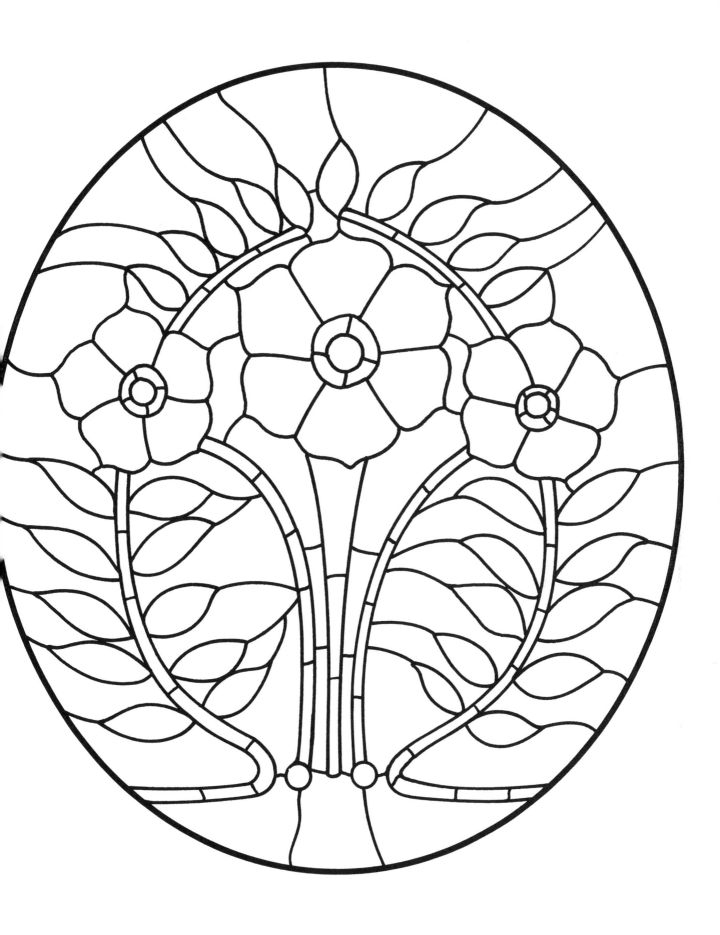

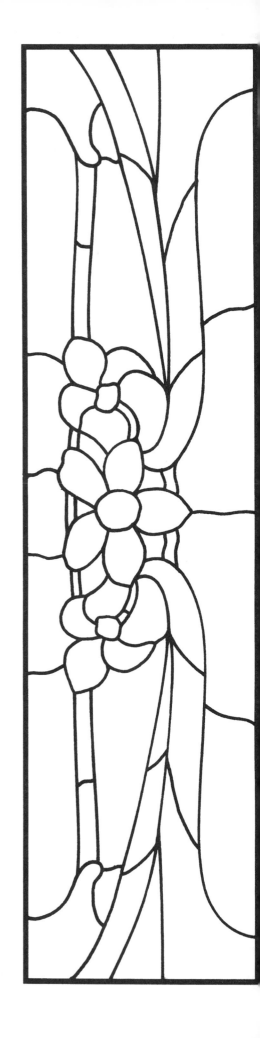

14

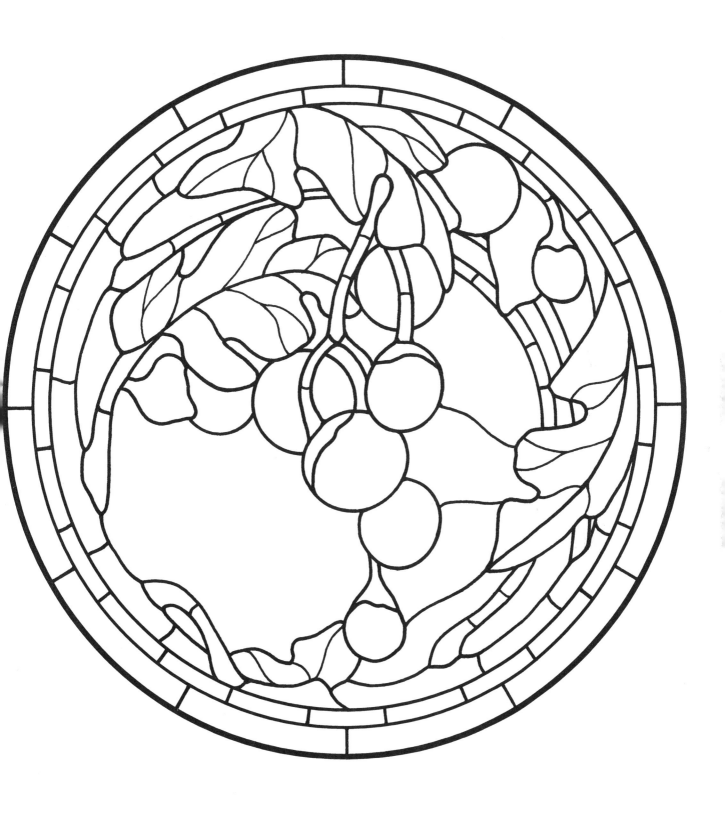

19

21

24

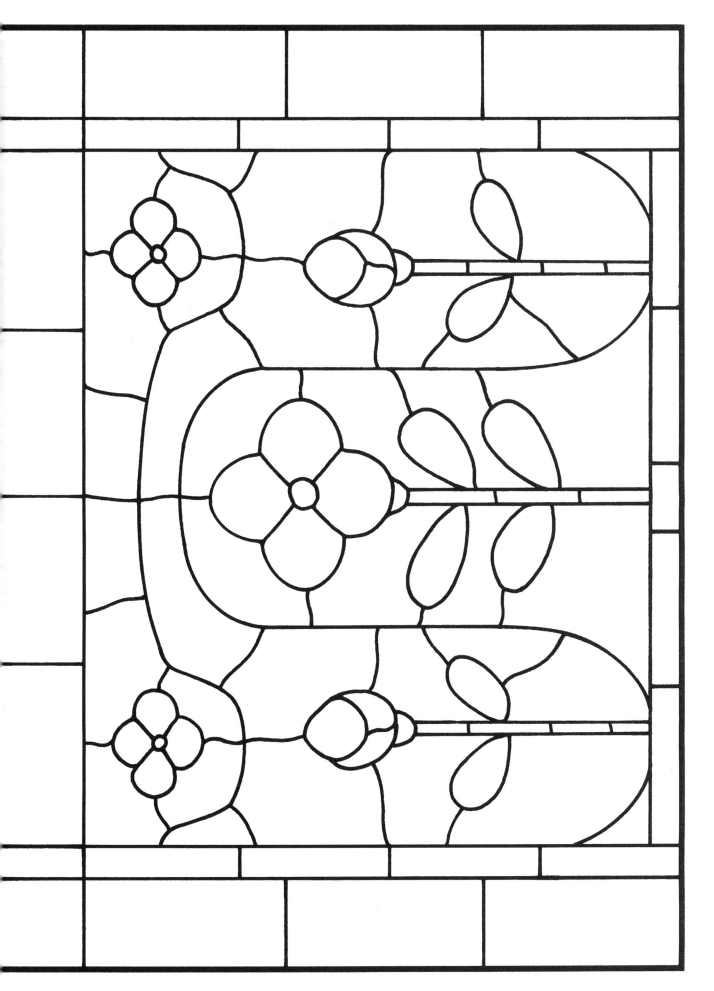

25

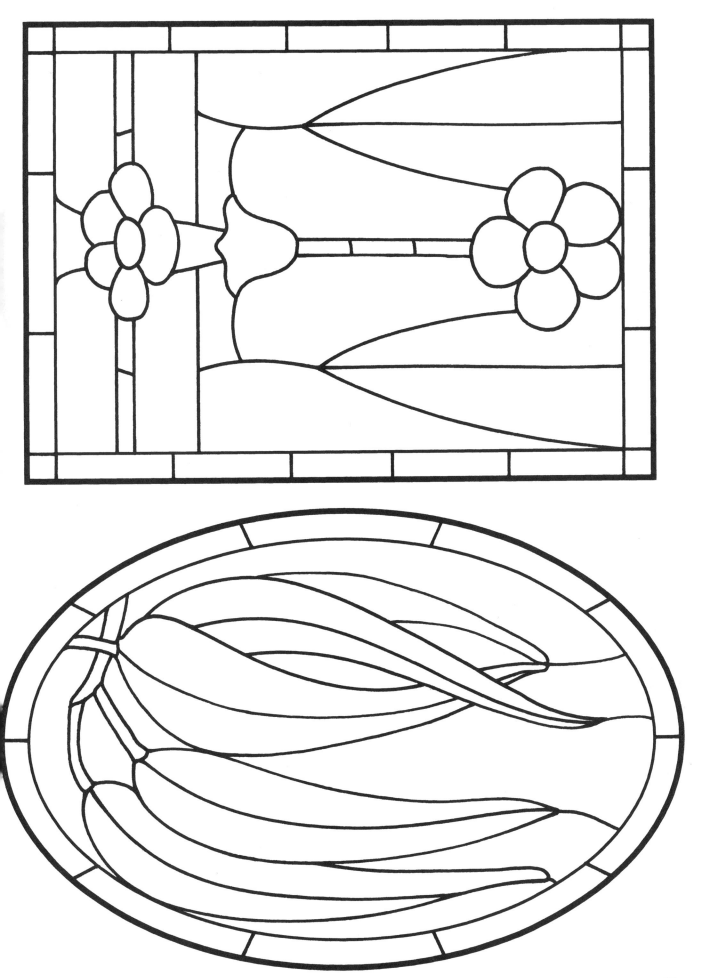

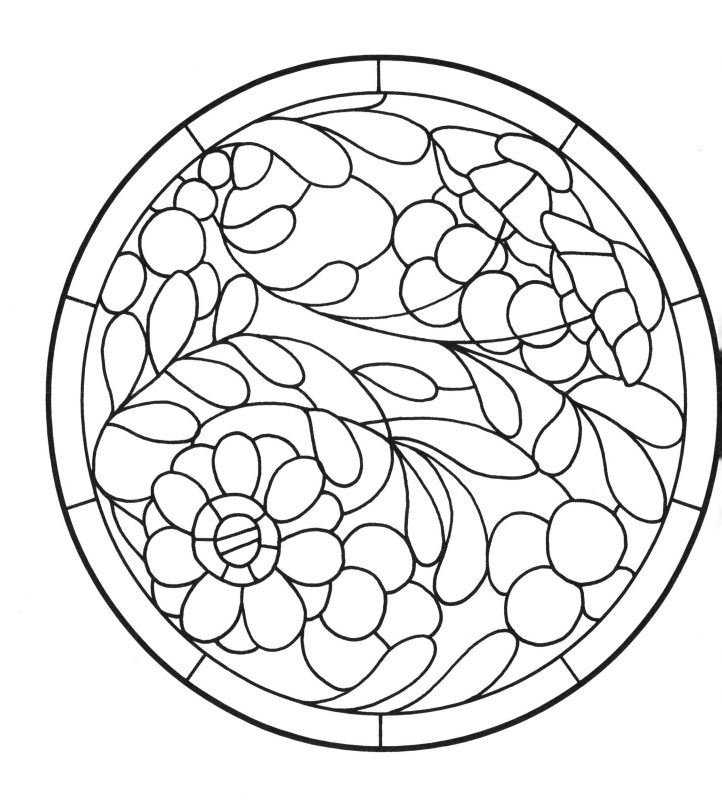

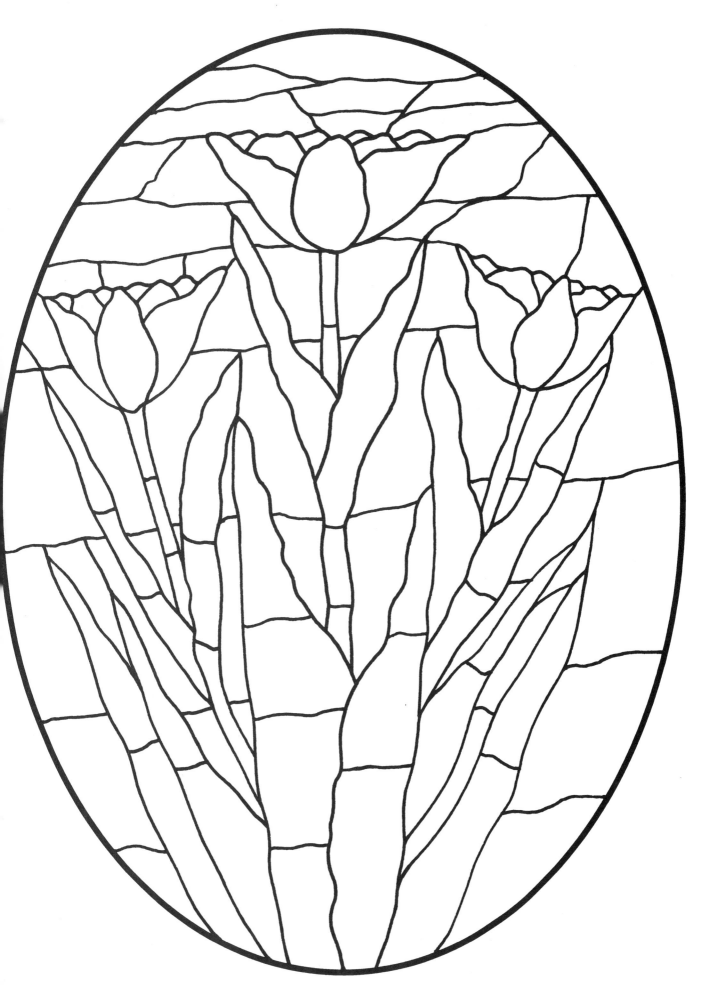

32

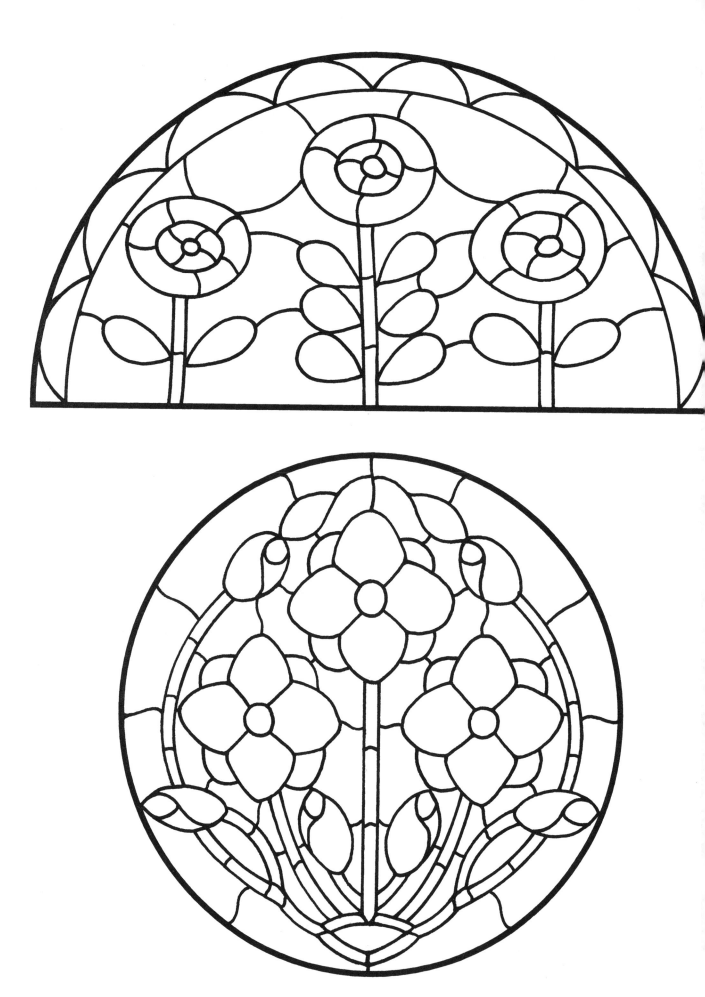

35

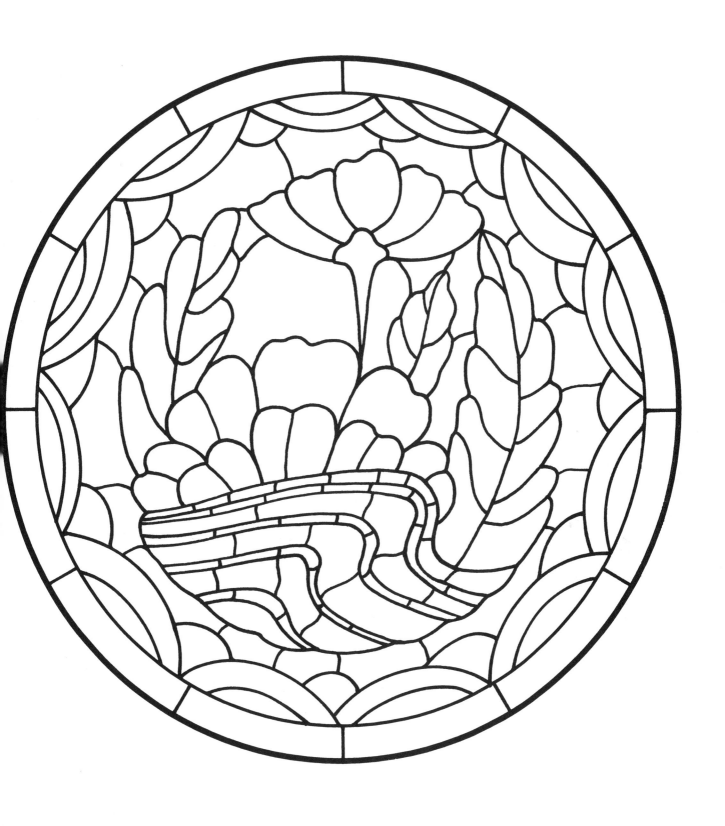

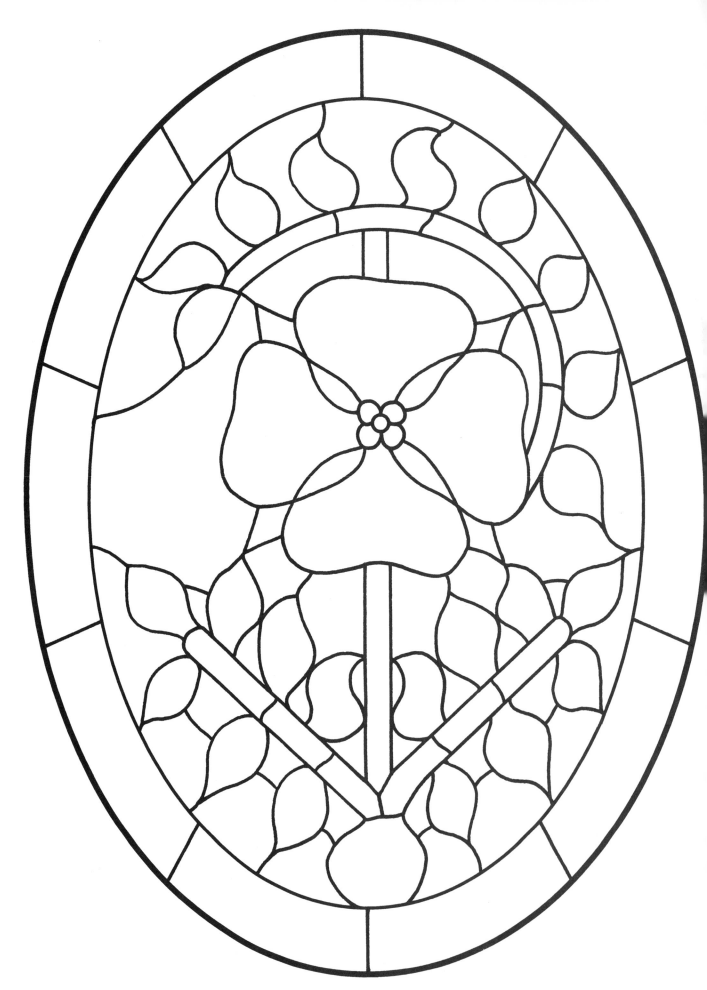

41

45

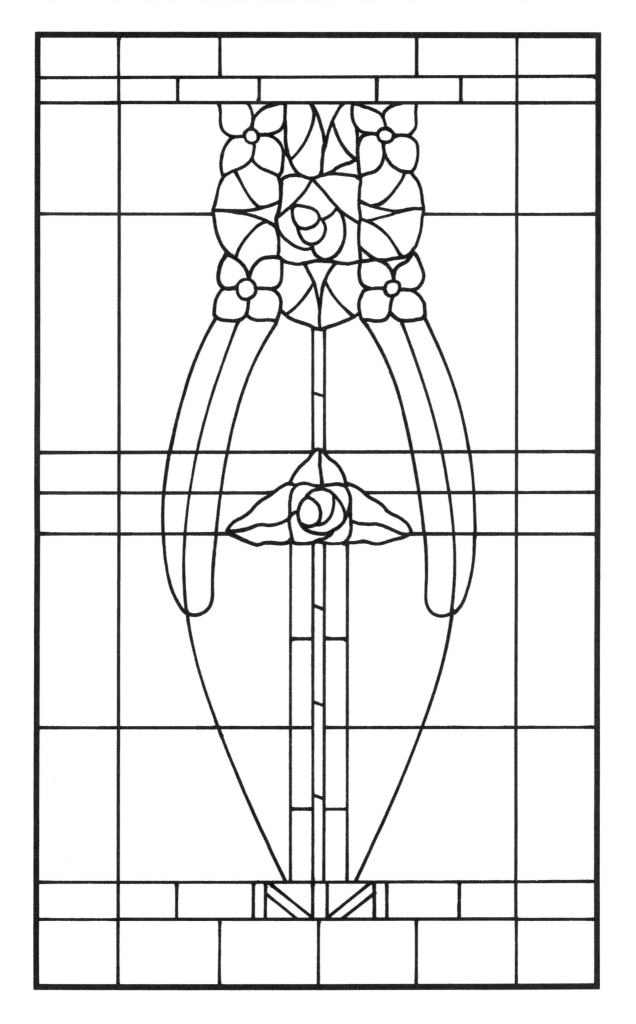

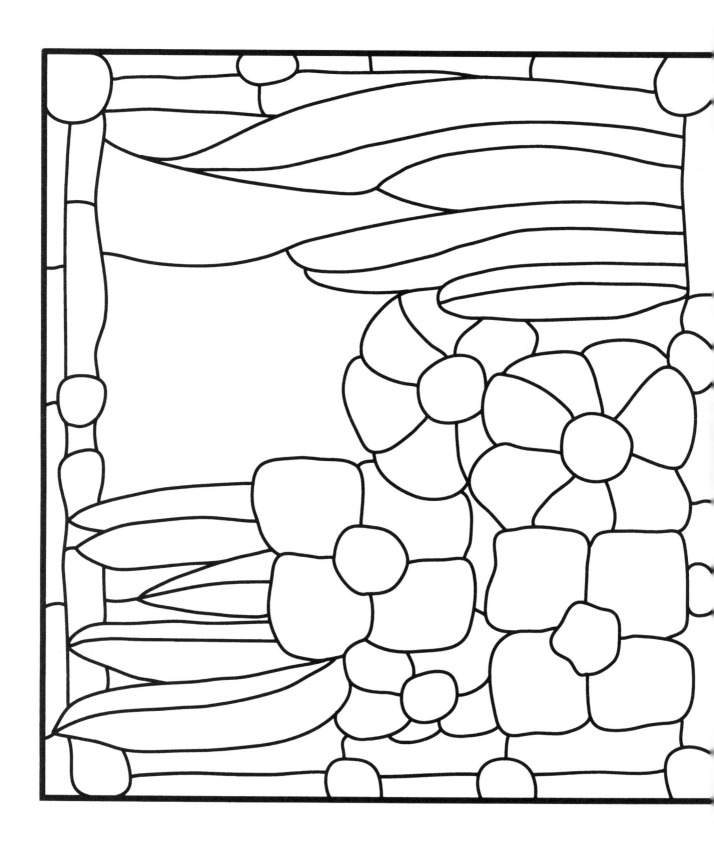

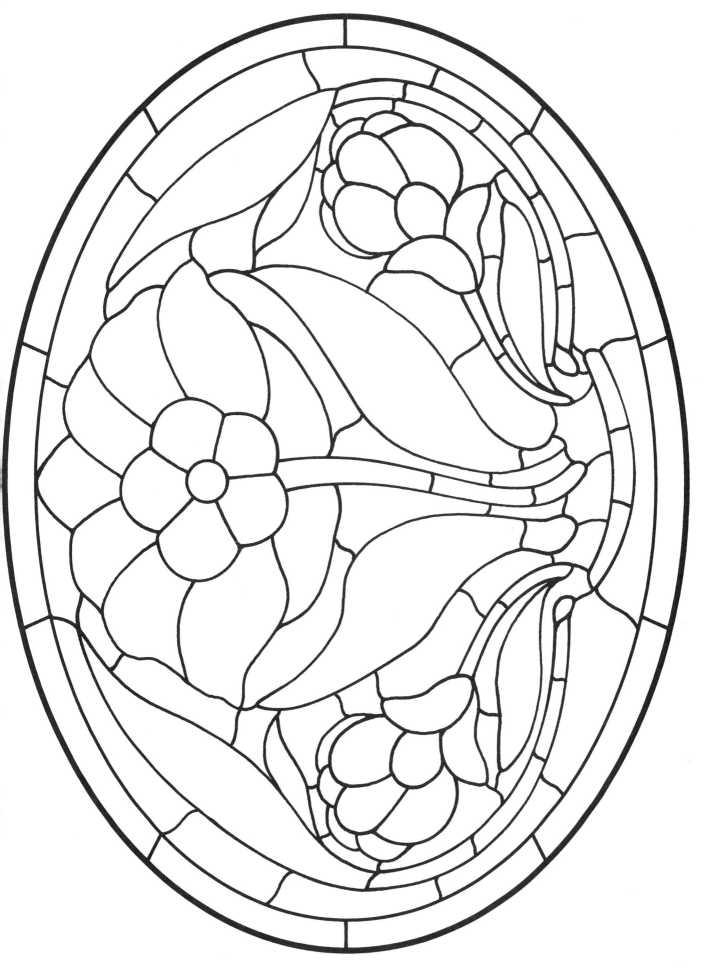

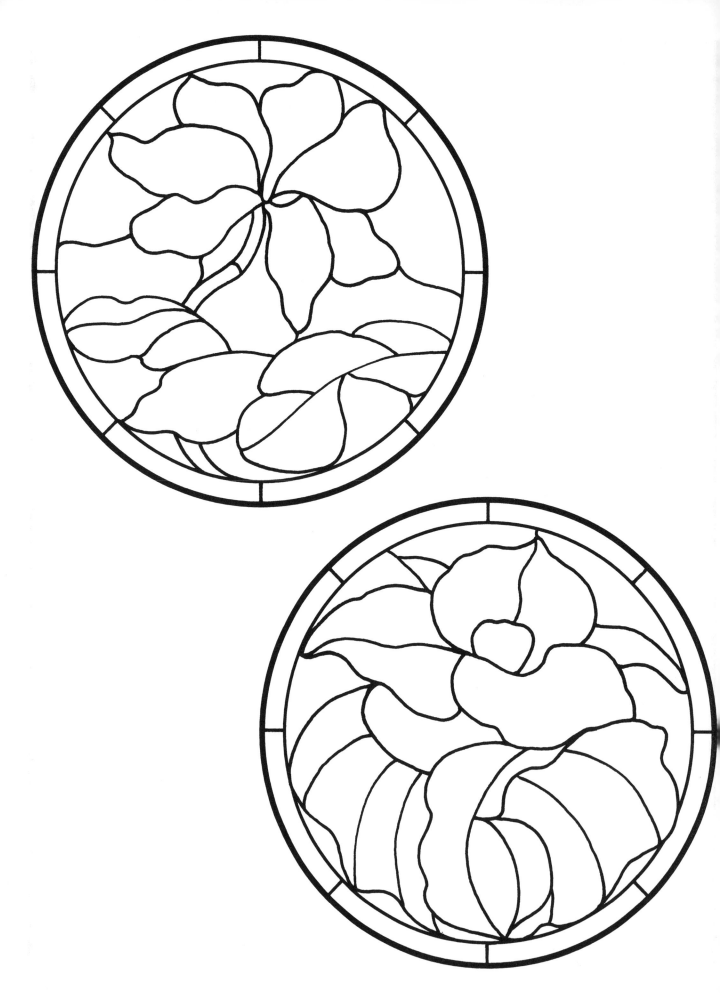

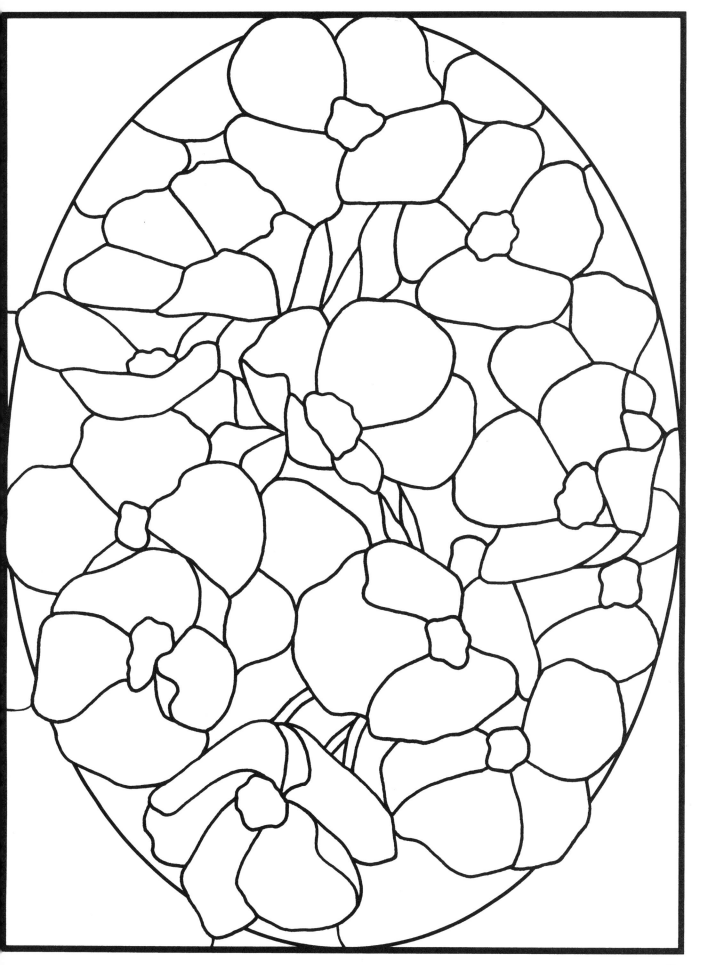

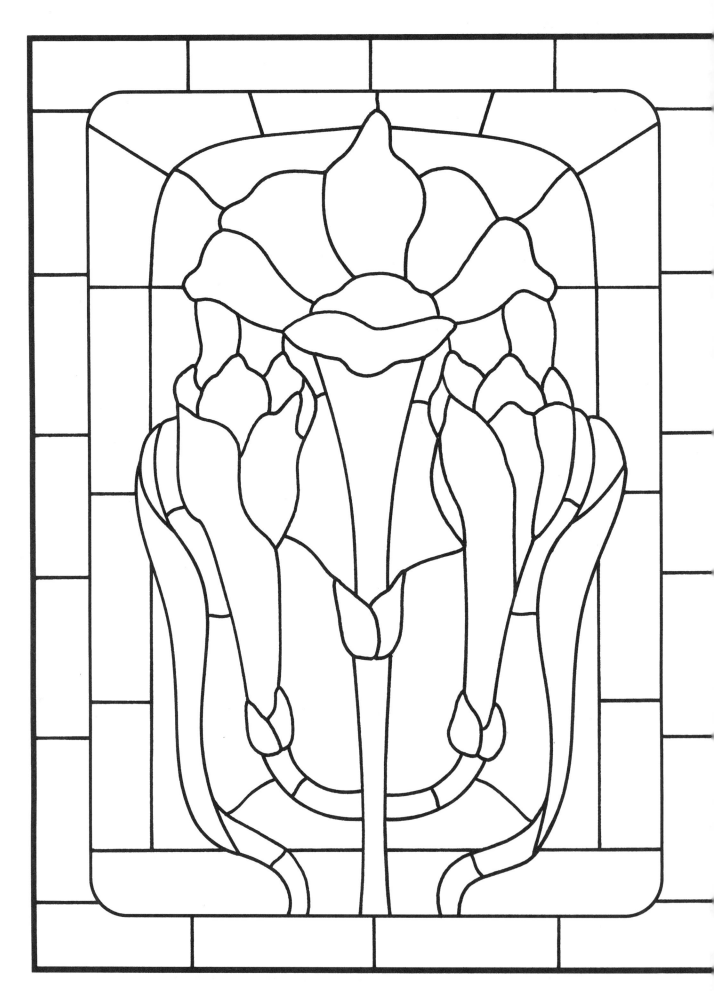

54

55

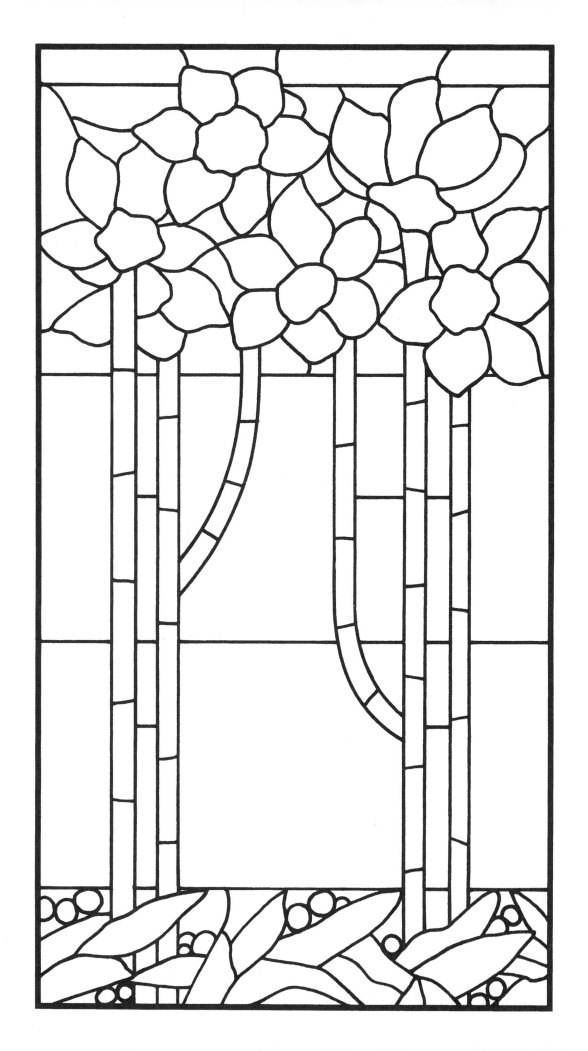

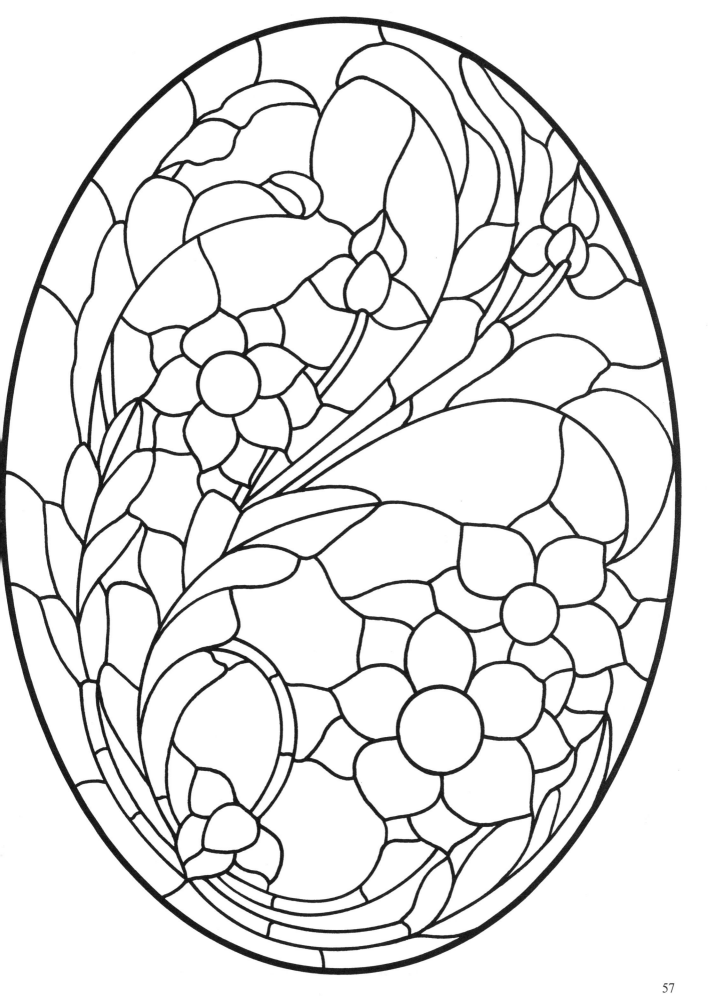

58